Bach's Cel Suites I - III Arranged for Tenor Banjo

by Rob MacKillop

1 2

Visit us on the Web at www.melbay.com — E-mail us at email@melbay.com

Contents

Bach's Cello Suites I - III
arranged for Tenor Banjo
by Rob MacKillop

Despite the cello's ability to sustain long notes, Bach's cello music is largely constructed of a line of continuous semiquavers, punctuated with occasional chords. It is this quality which the tenor banjo excels at. And as the two instruments share the same tuning, albeit an octave apart, it struck me that it would be worth exploring Bach's cello suites on the tenor banjo, and I have to say that I think these three suites work magnificently.

Many years ago I played these suites on the guitar, then more recently on the baroque lute. It might surprise many of my guitar and lute colleagues when I declare that I think they work better on the tenor banjo.

We have two tenor banjo tunings in common use today: Standard [CGDA] and Irish [GDAE] and as long as one is playing from the TAB score, either one will do. Standard tuning will provide sparkle to the faster pieces, while Irish will give more of a sombre mood to the slower pieces. For the recording of the 1st suite, I actually tuned Standard down a minor third, as I felt that pitch gave the best results on the banjo I was playing [Deering Eagle II], in the style I wished to play. But any pitch will do. I also play these suites on a cello banjo at cello pitch, with impressive results.

A 'Suite' is a collection of dances of varying speeds and time signatures, conceived to be performed as a whole, and preceded by a Prelude. Bach's Prelude to the 1st suite here is magnificent and justly famous. He starts by simply outlining the Tonic, Dominant and Sub Dominant chords, before modulating to the Dominant. He then spends half of the entire piece returning from the Dominant to the Tonic. It couldn't be more simple, yet it holds the interest throughout.

Each note has meaning in a harmonic context. Each single note is either outlining a chord, or moving to another chord. In this arrangement I have not taken out or added a single note. This is exactly what Bach wrote. Your role as interpreter is to shape the lines and help give a sense of forward movement, pausing here and there to catch a breath. This is subtle music, requiring a subtle technique. Downbeats must have down strokes, upbeats, upstrokes. It's a simple rule, though one not always easy to execute. Your downstrokes should be subtly stronger than your upstrokes, as this helps to articulate the harmonic movement and melodic phrasing.

INSTRUMENTS

All of these suites can be played on a regular tenor banjo, but for this recording I decided to use three very different banjos...

Suite No. 1 - For this suite I used a magnificent Deering Eagle II Tenor Banjo. The 2010 tone ring used in this banjo helps provide a beautifully warm and clear sound, capable of playing brilliantly in many musical situations. A classic 21st-century banjo. To increase the resonance for this music for the recording, I detuned the banjo by a minor third.

Suite No. 2 - Here I used a beautiful gourd tenor banjo made for me by Jason Smith of JaybirdBanjos. Banjos having a sound chamber made from a dried out gourd came to America via the slave trade, and as such resonate with a sound heard in the time of Bach. The gourd banjo used here is tuned in what is often described as Irish tuning, GDAE, although that tuning was used also by early jazz musicians in the States.

Suite No. 3 - The cello banjo was a common addition to early 20th-century banjo orchestras. It seems an obvious candidate for Bach's cello music, being tuned the same way and at the same low pitch. Gold Tone have created a beautiful modern version of this deep 4-string, which is a delight to play.

Please check out my website, RobMacKillop.net for more information, pictures of the instruments, and videos, and feel free to contact me from there if you have any questions or comments.

Rob MacKillop
Edinburgh
2013

Bach's First Cello Suite
arranged for Tenor or Cello Banjo

Prelude

Track 1

Arranged by Rob MacKillop

J. S. Bach

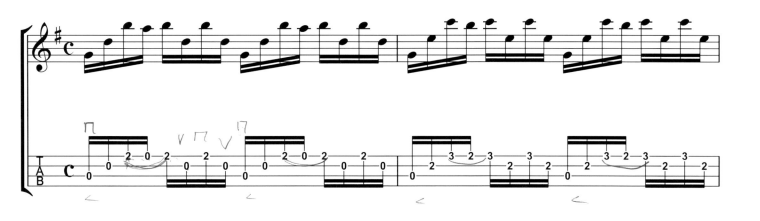

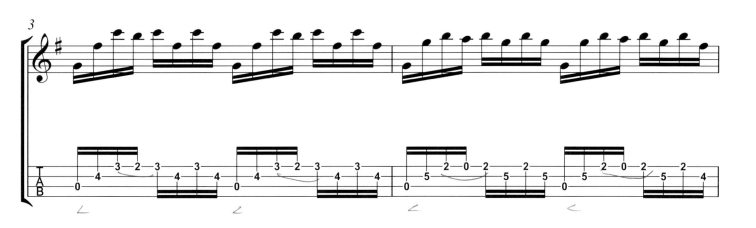

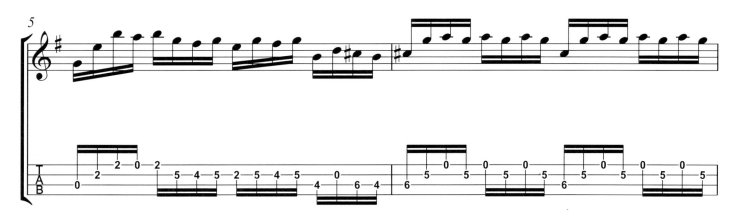

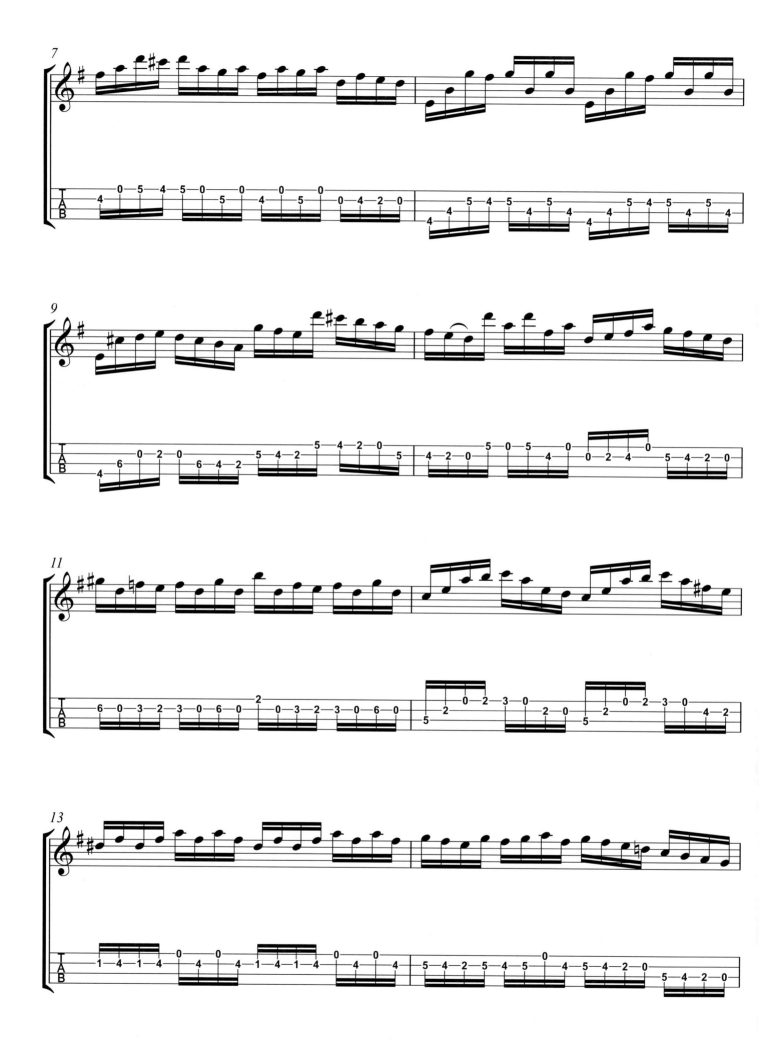

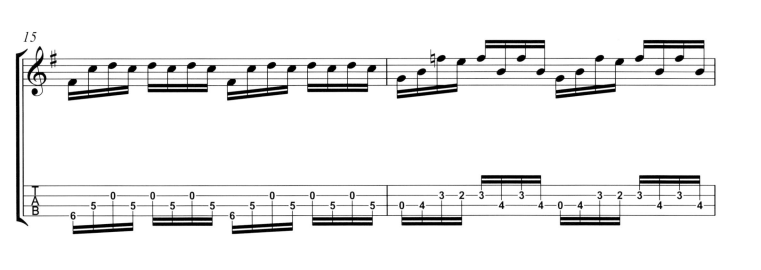

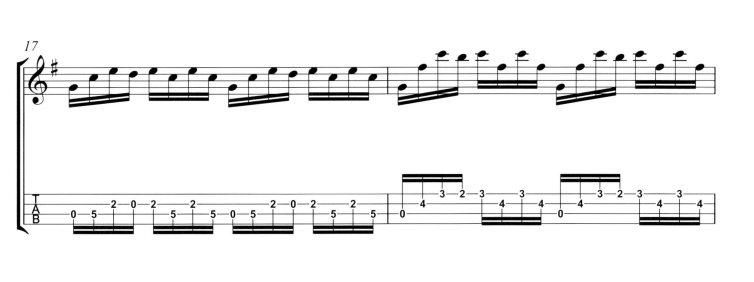

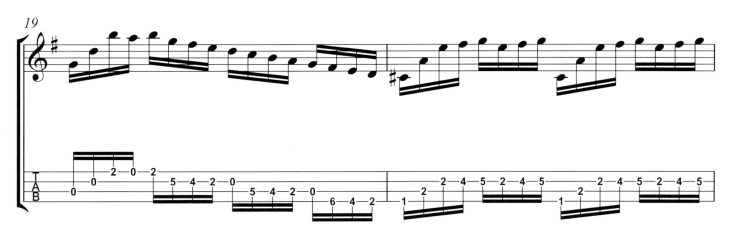

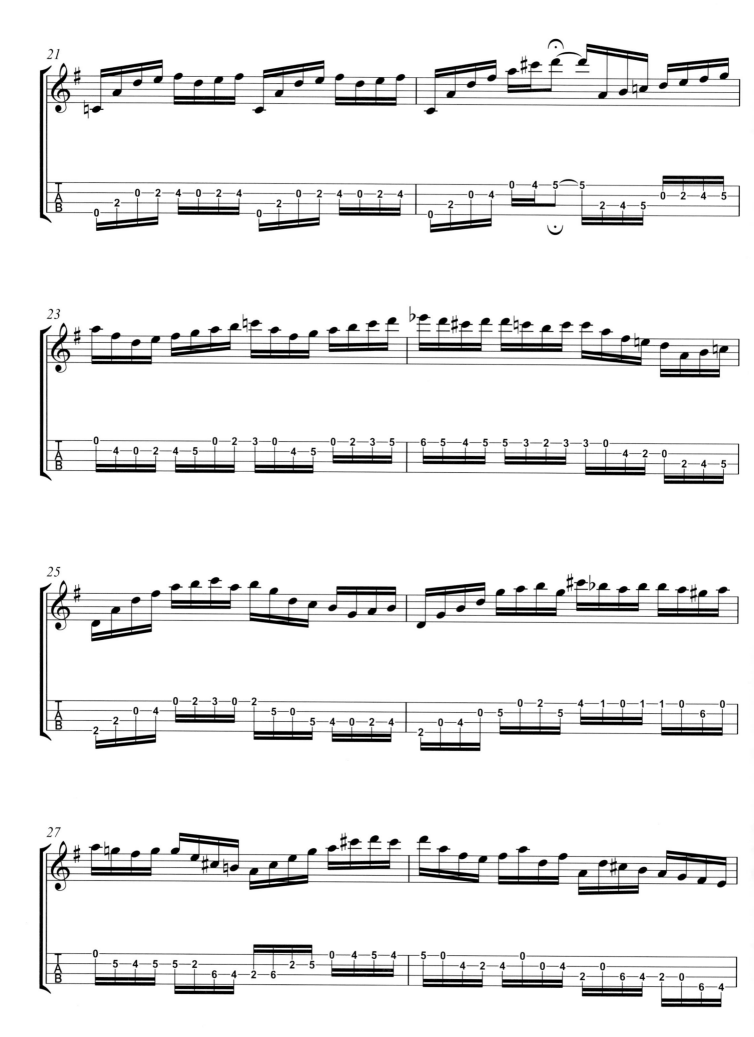

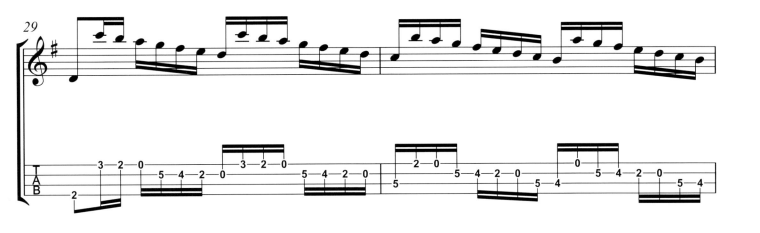

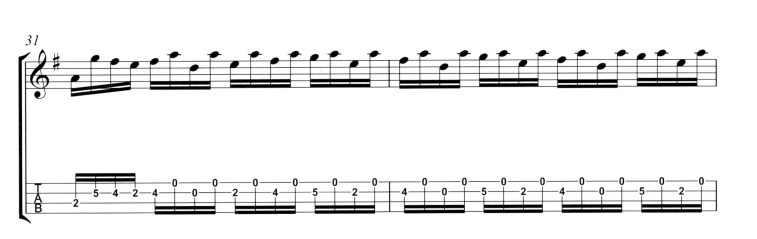

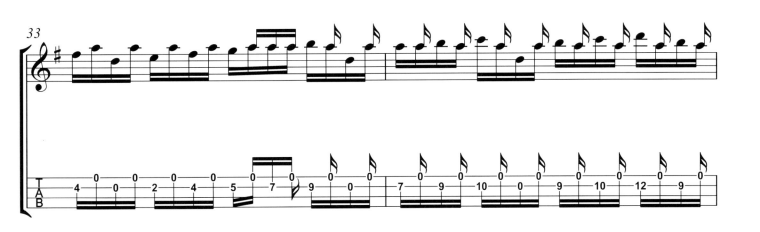

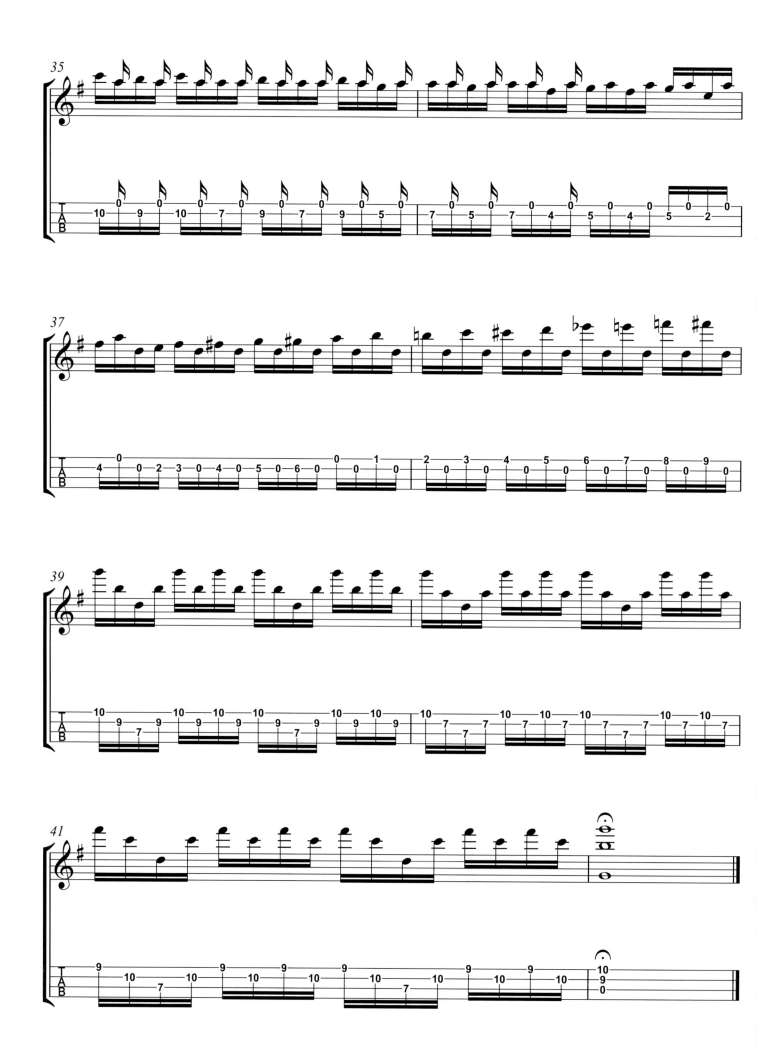

Allemande

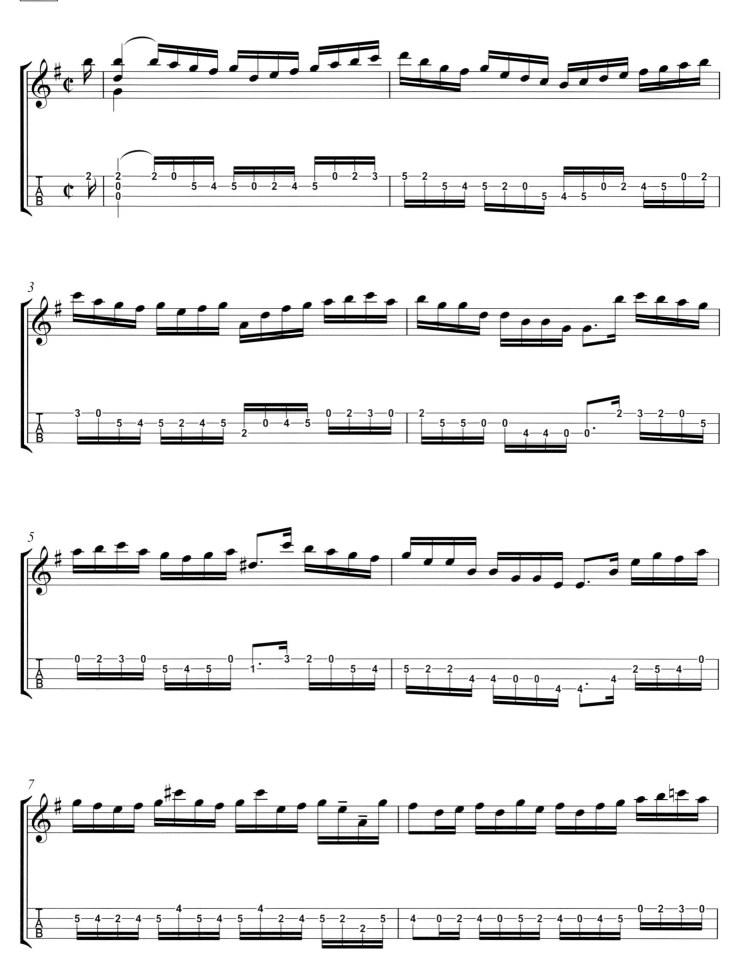

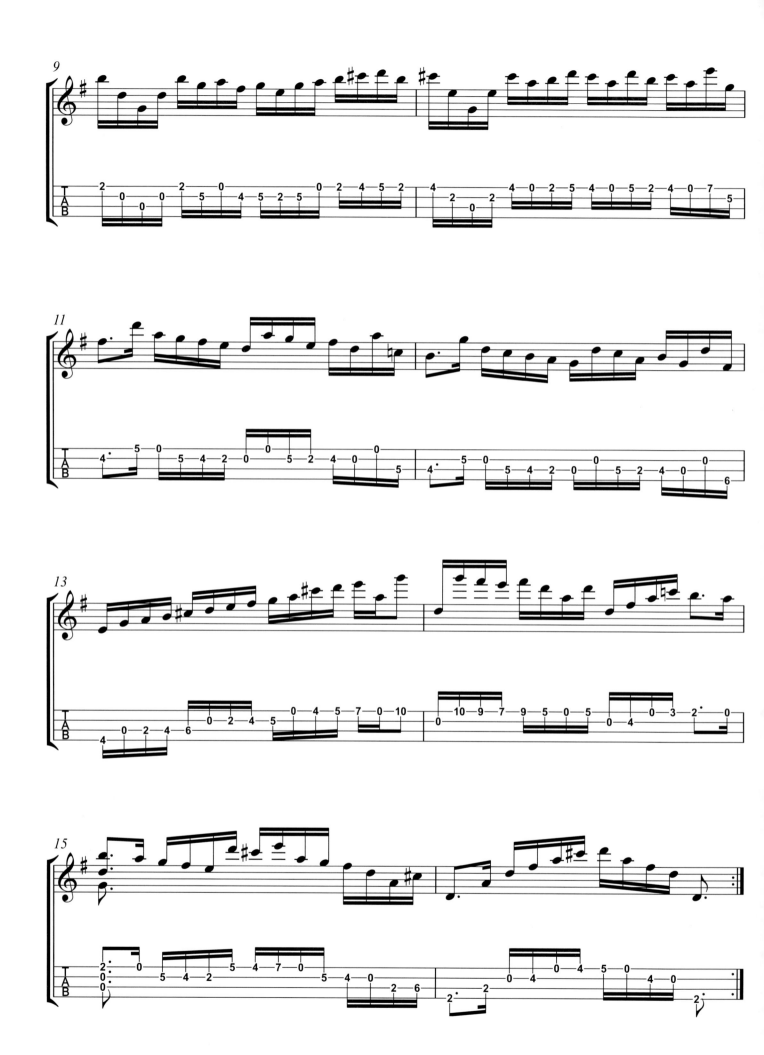

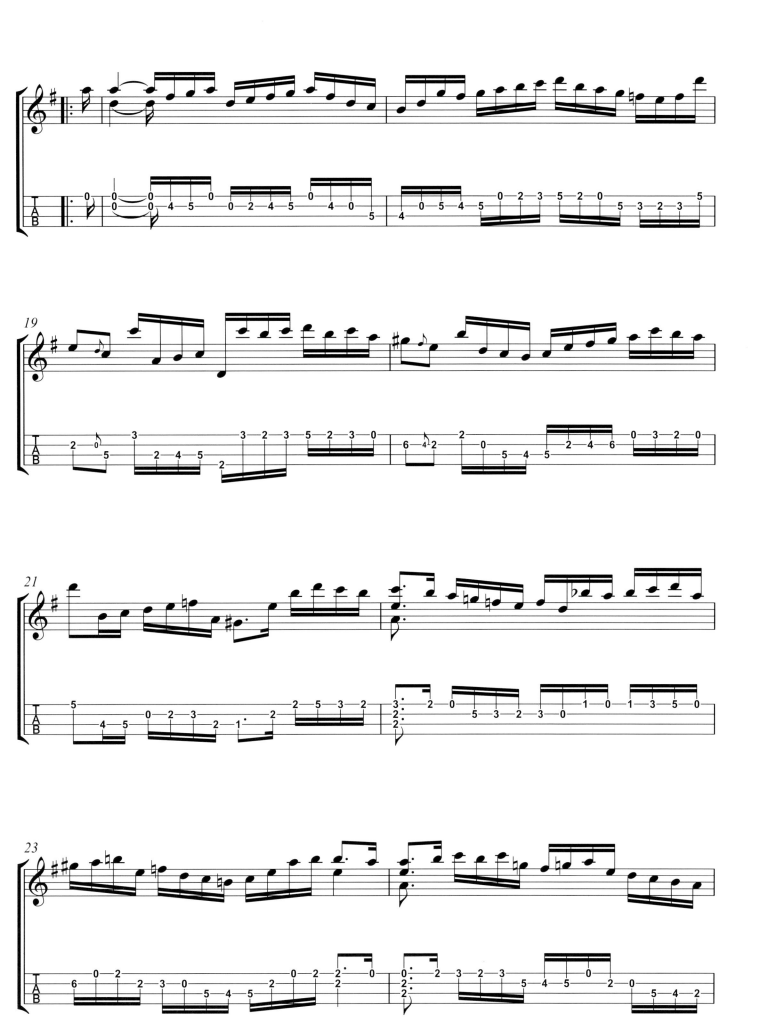

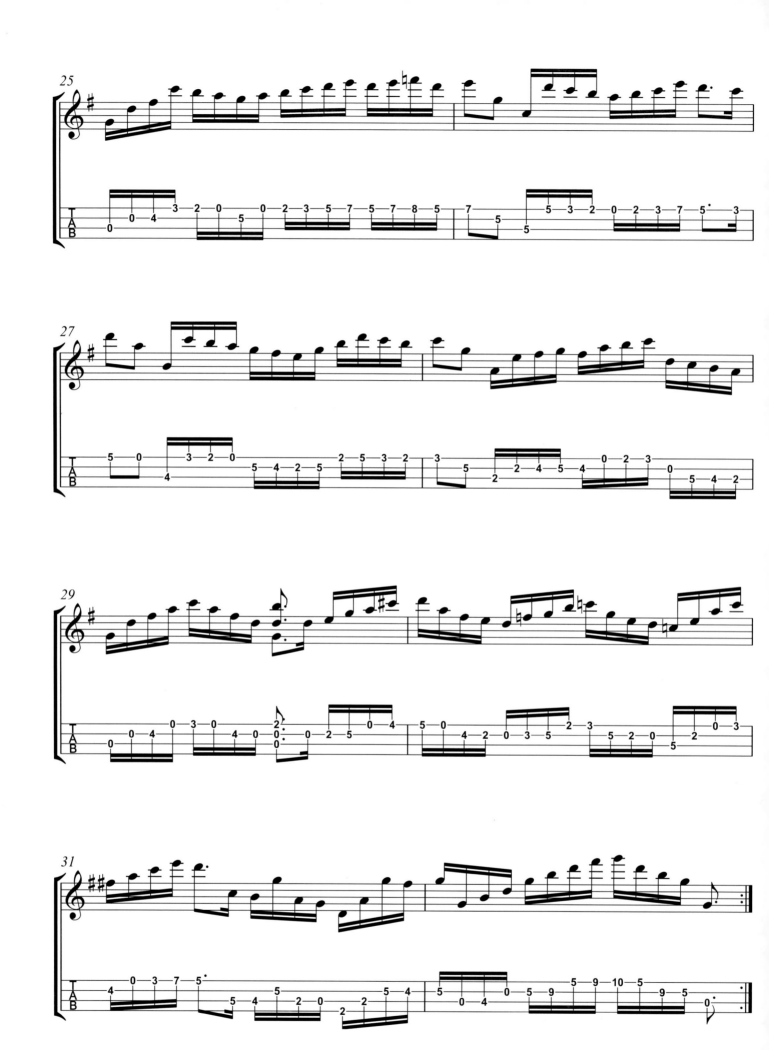

14

Courante

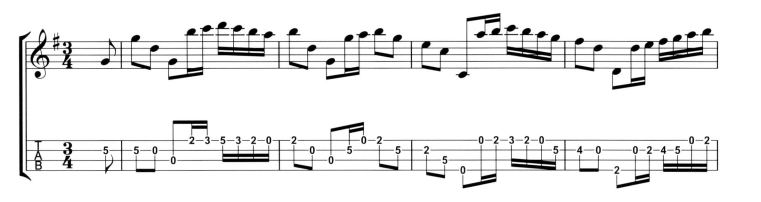

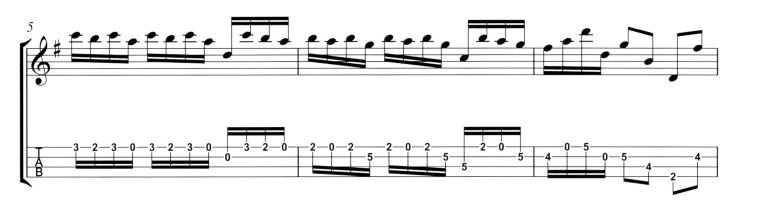

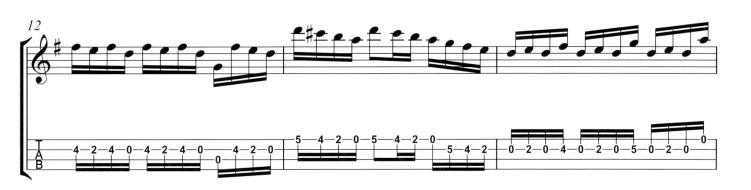

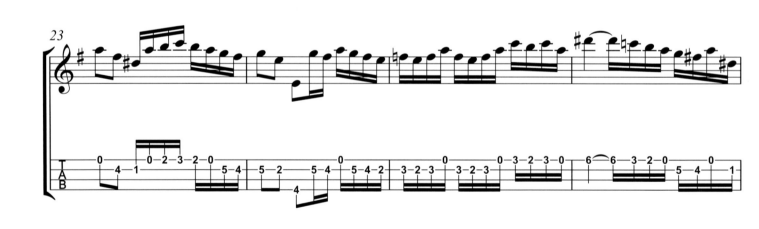

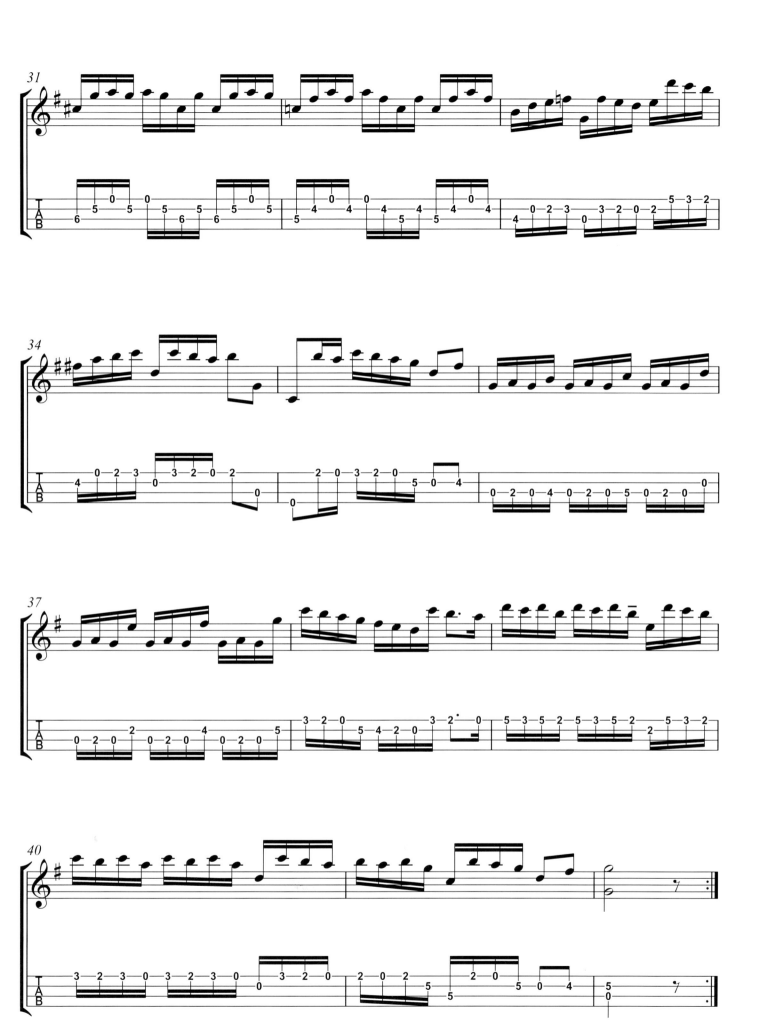

Sarabande

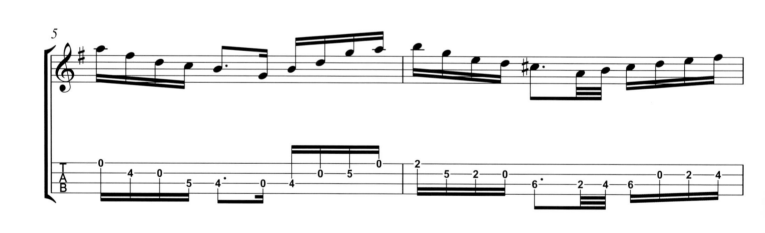

Minuet I

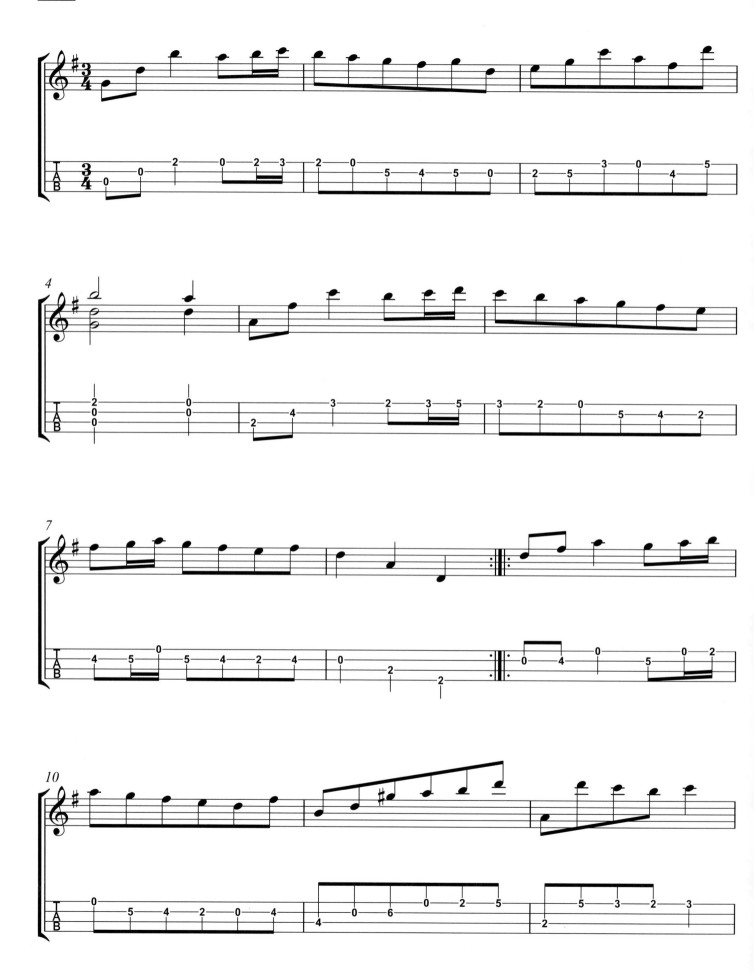

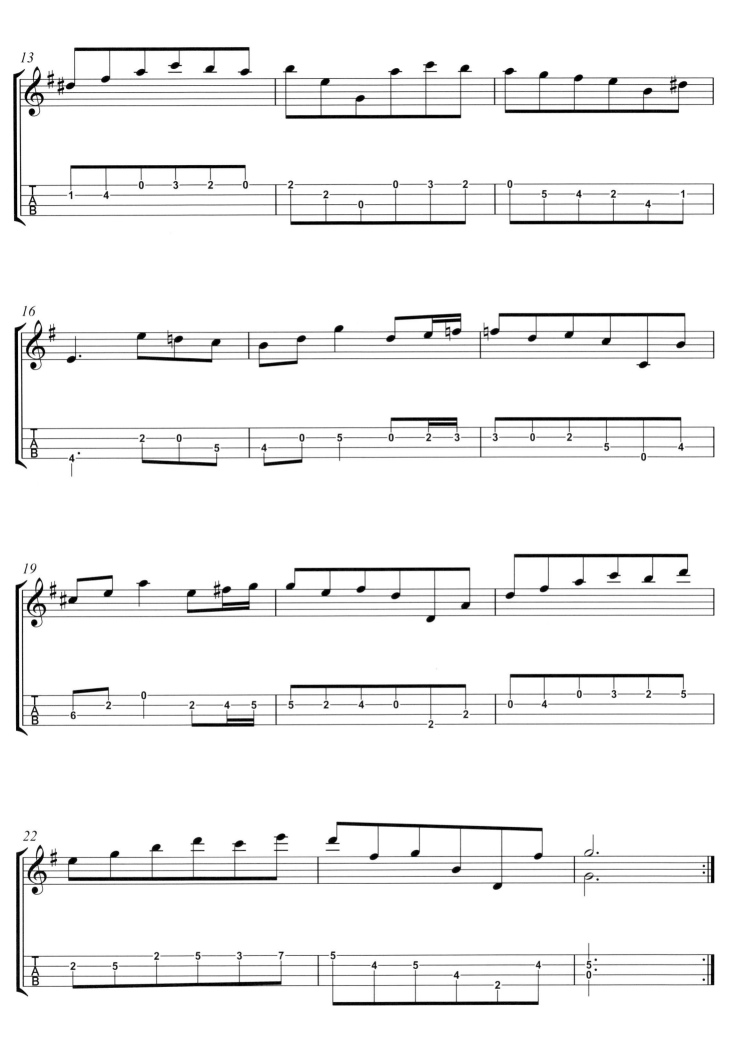

Minuet II

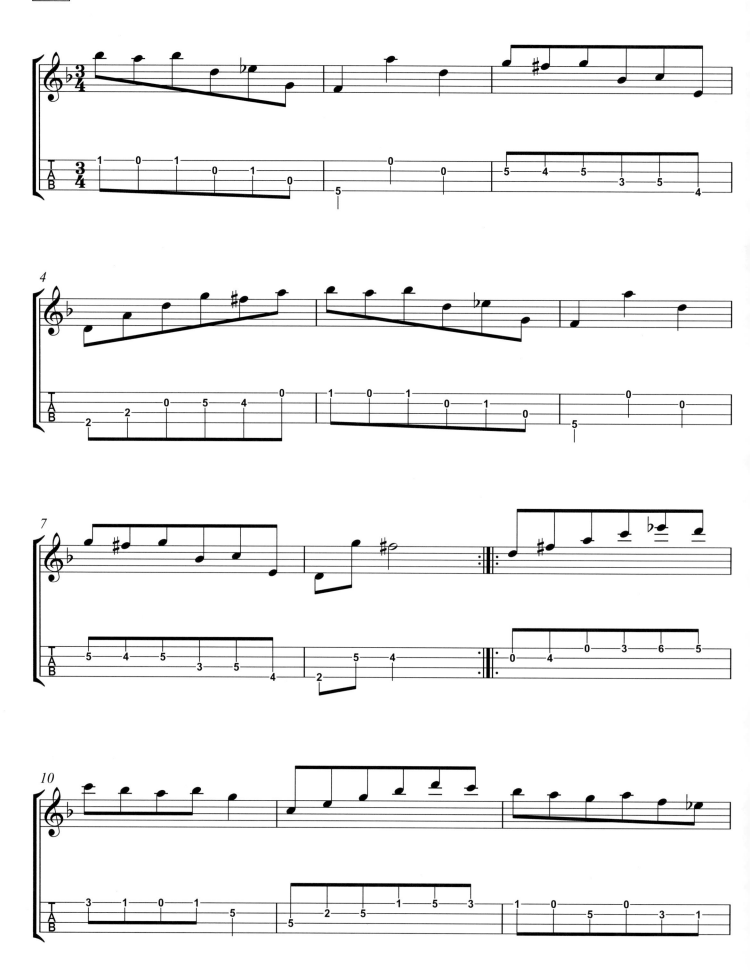

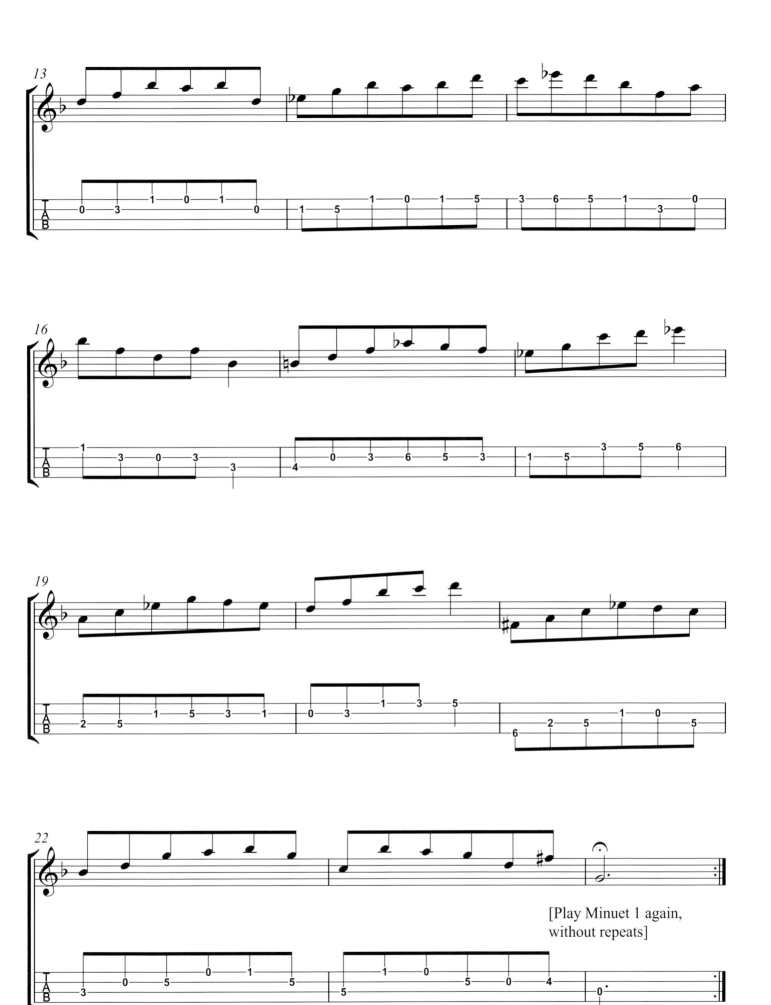

[Play Minuet 1 again,
without repeats]

23

Gigue

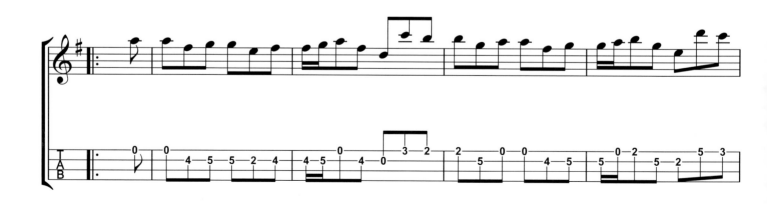

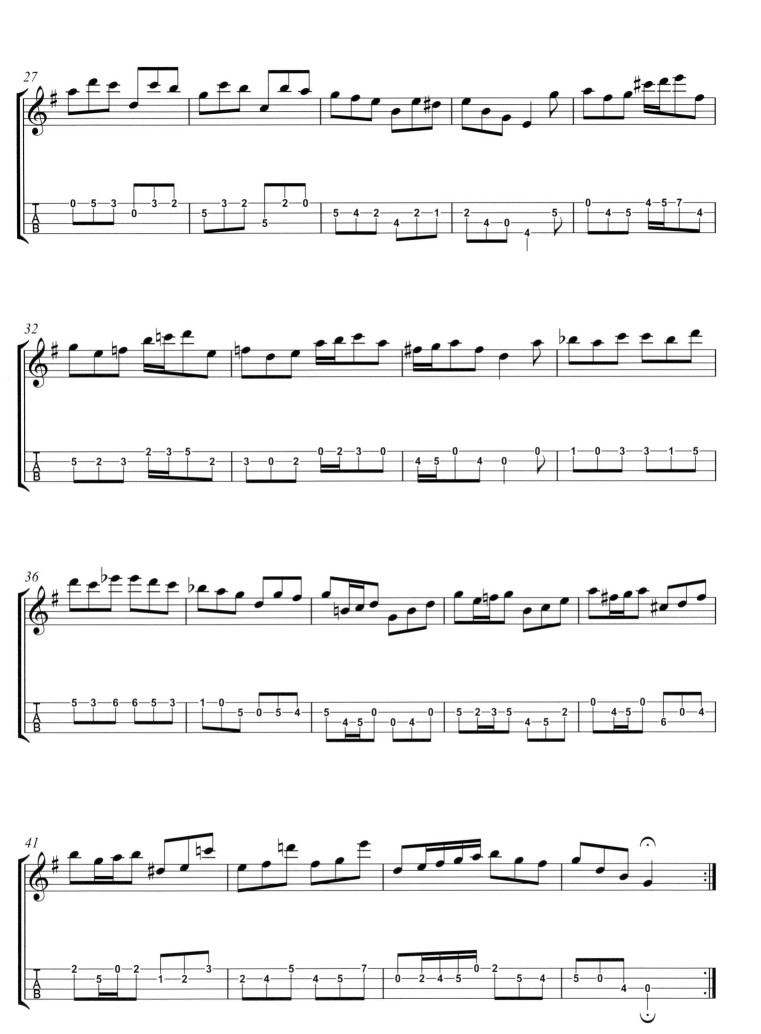

25

Bach's Second Cello Suite
arranged for Tenor Banjo

Prelude

Track 7

Arranged by Rob MacKillop

J. S. Bach

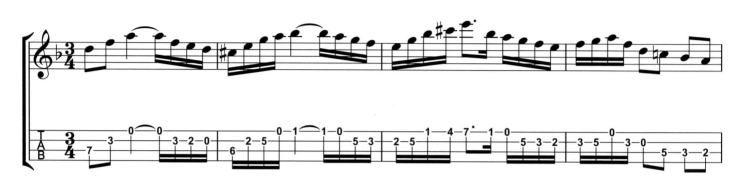

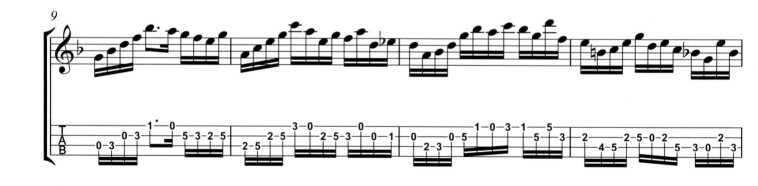

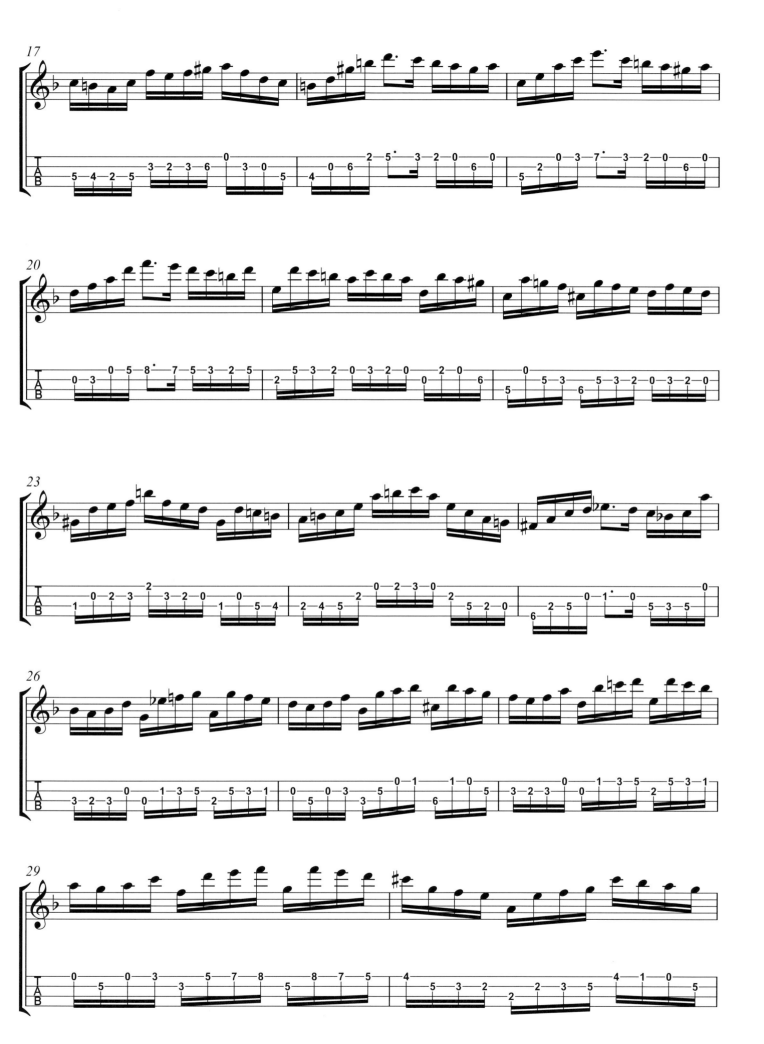

28

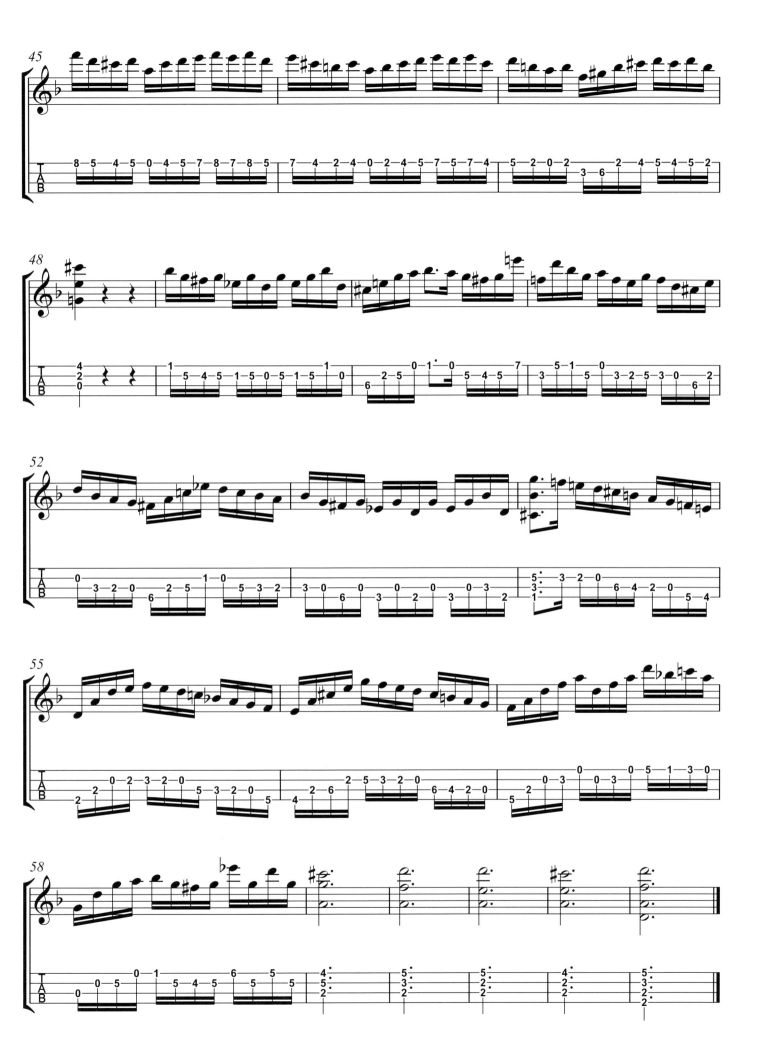

29

Allemande

31

Courante

Track 9

32

33

Sarabande

Minuet I

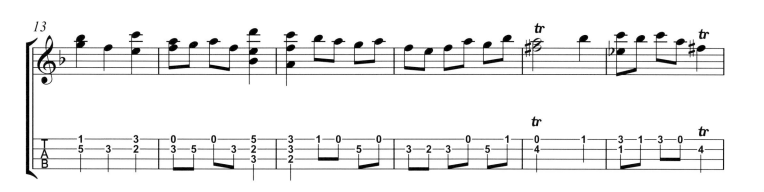

Minuet II

Gigue

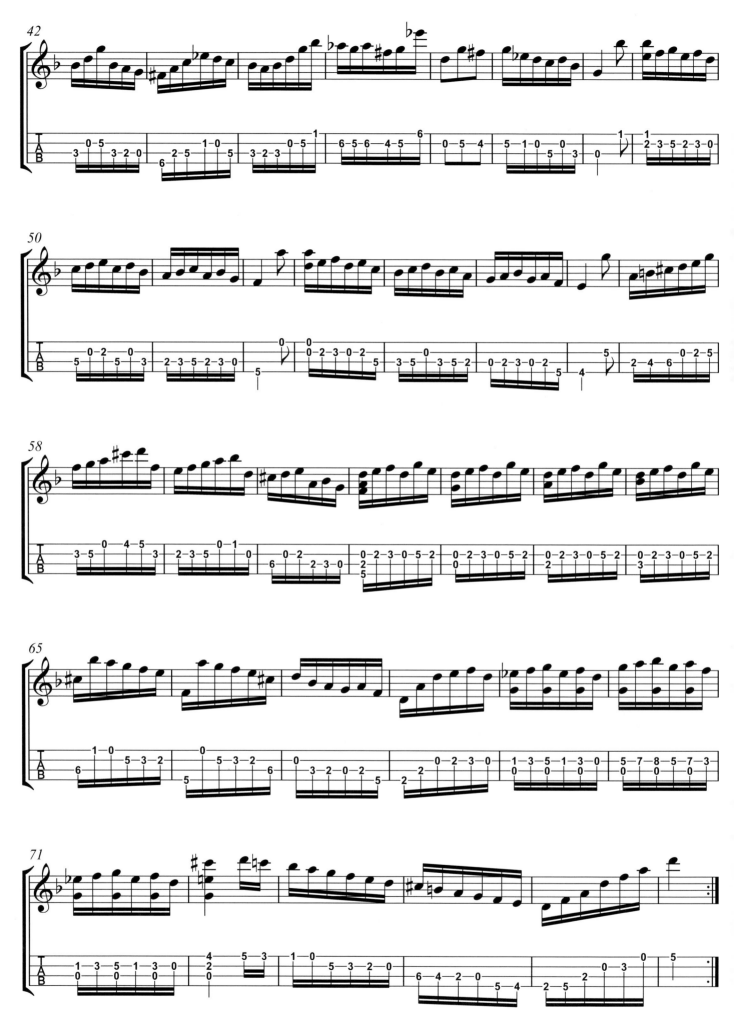

38

Bach's Third Cello Suite
arranged for Tenor or Cello Banjo

Prelude

Track 13

Arranged by Rob MacKillop

J. S. Bach

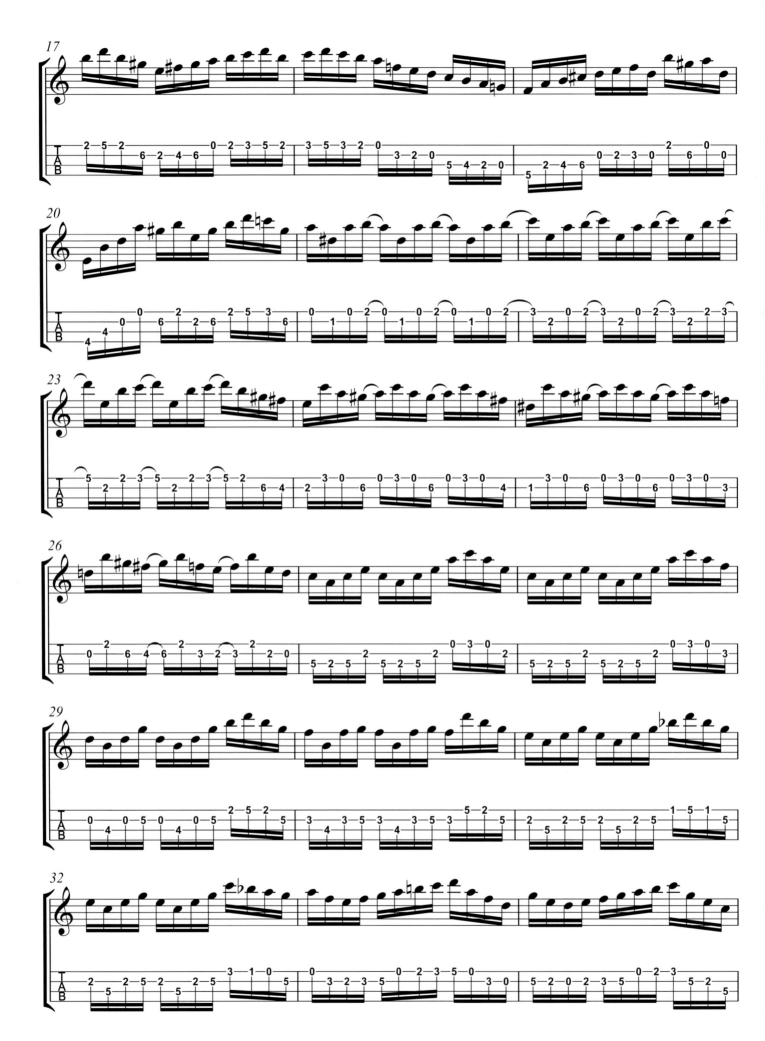

40

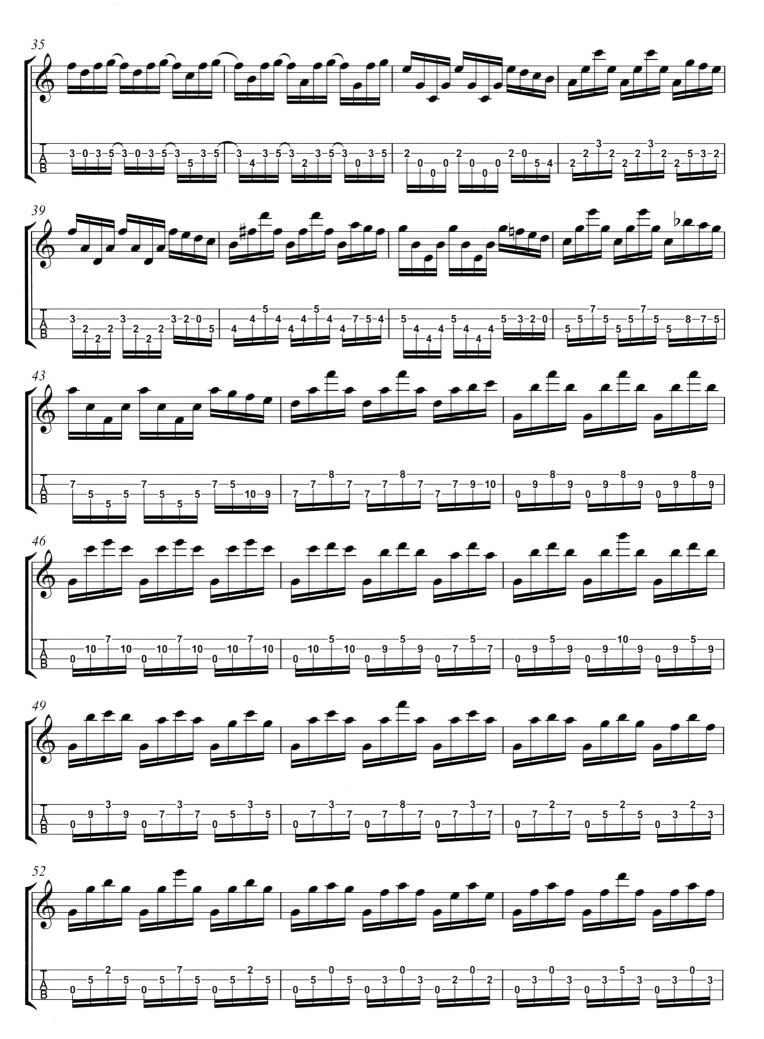

Allemande

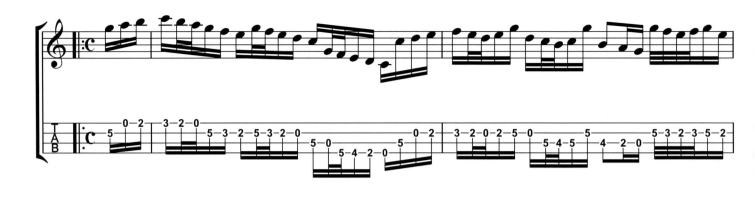

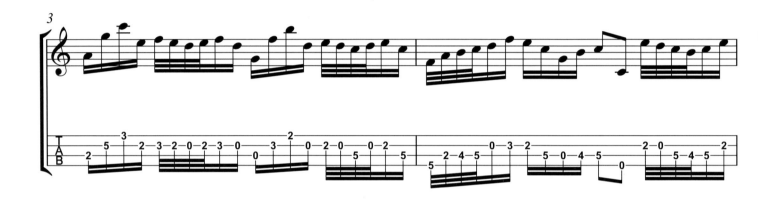

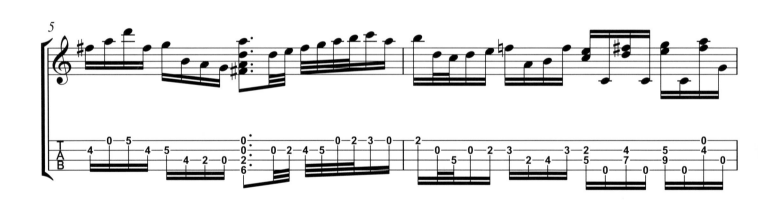

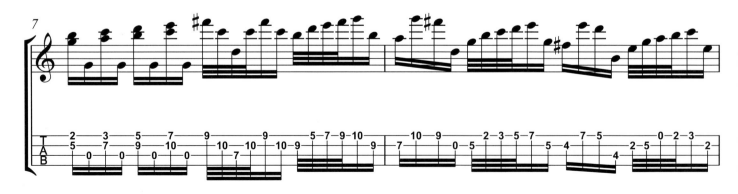

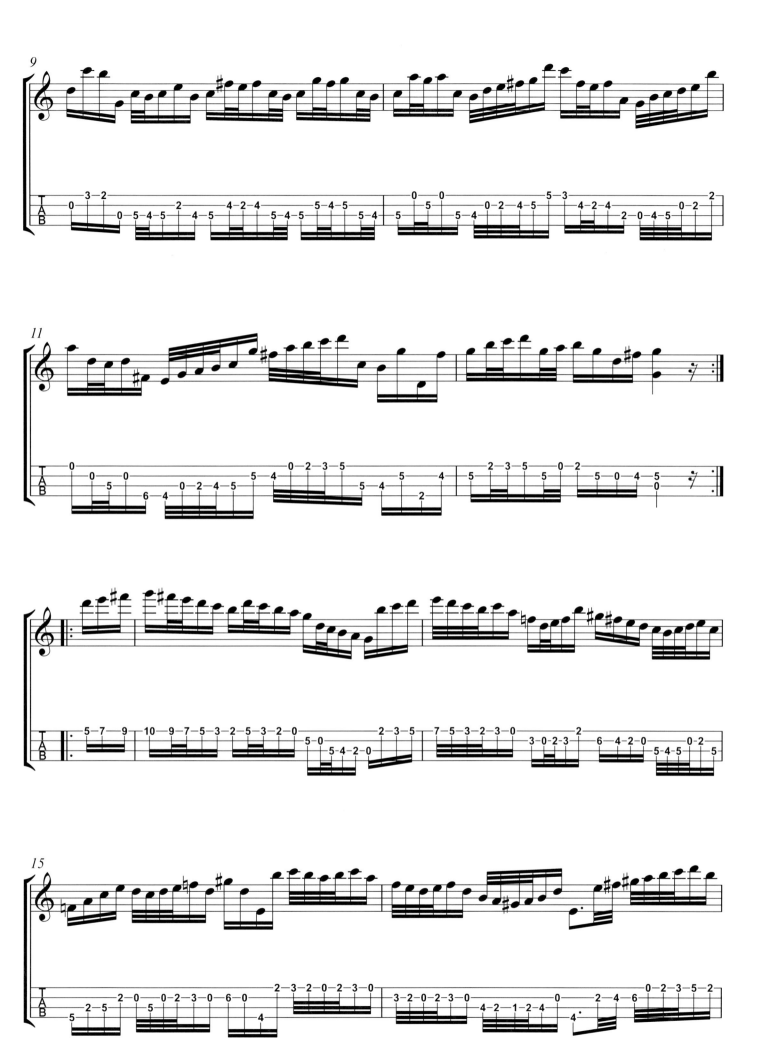

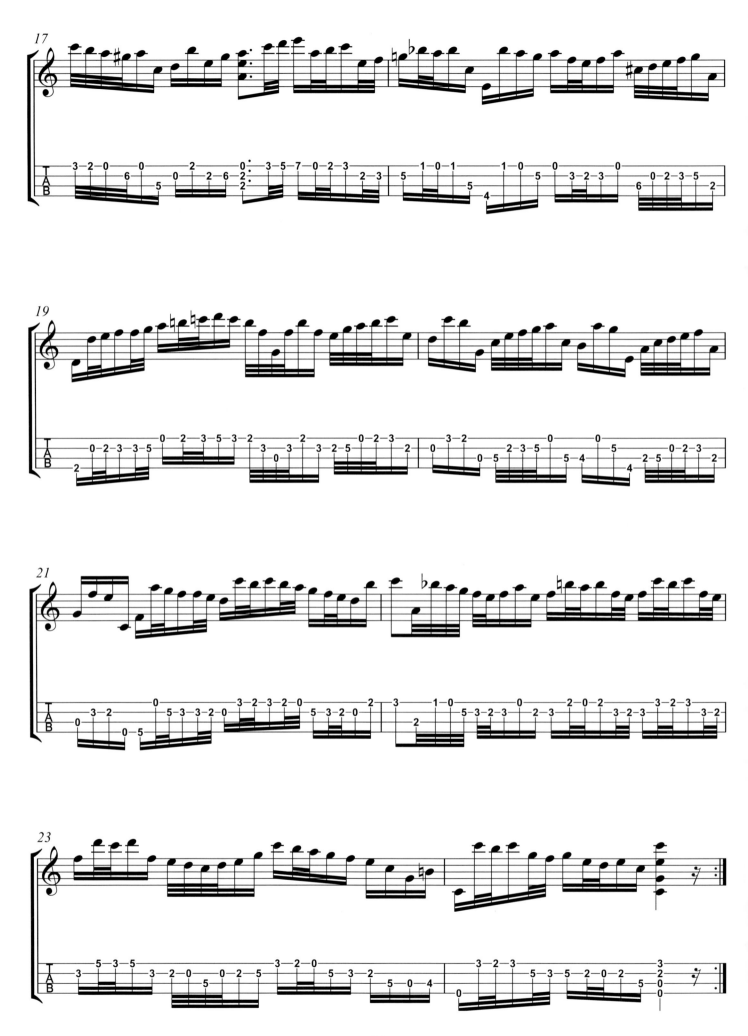

Courante

48

Sarabande

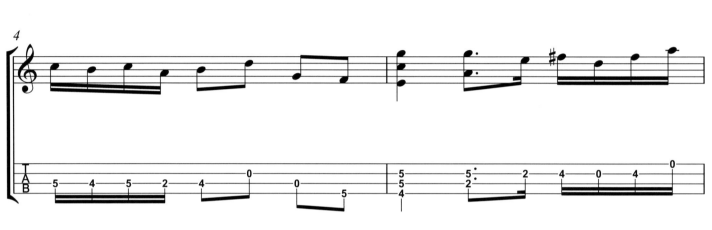

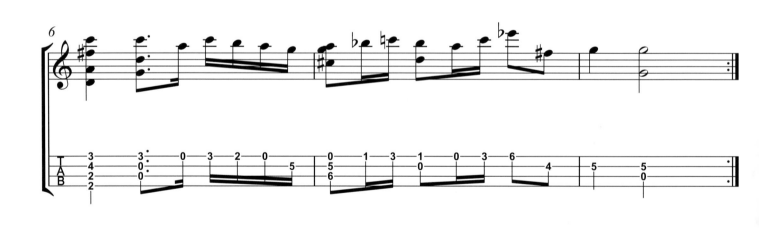

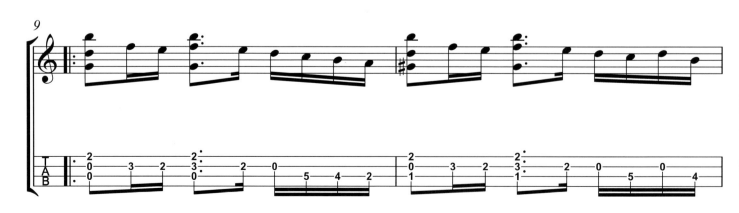

Bourrée I

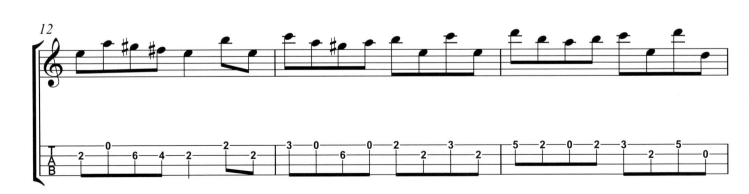

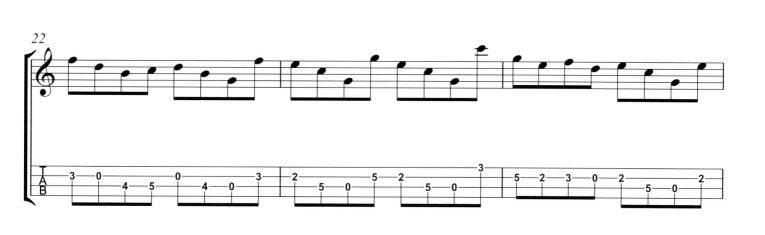

Bourrée II

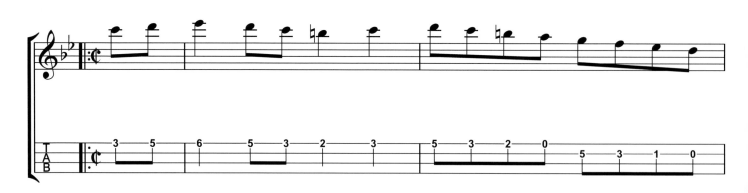

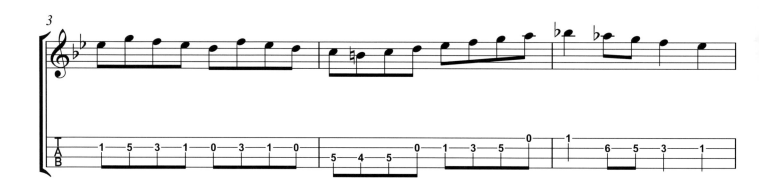

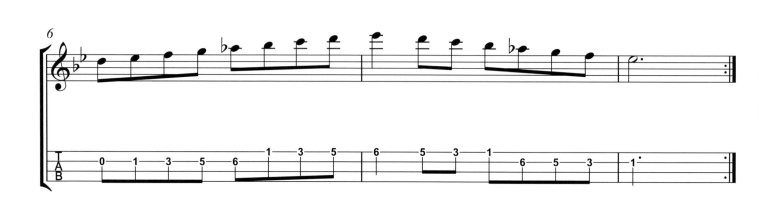

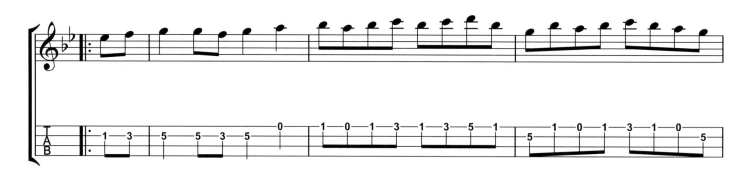

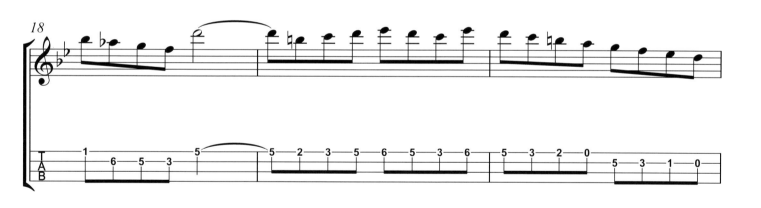

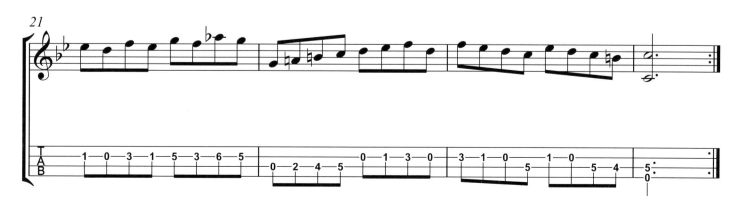

Gigue

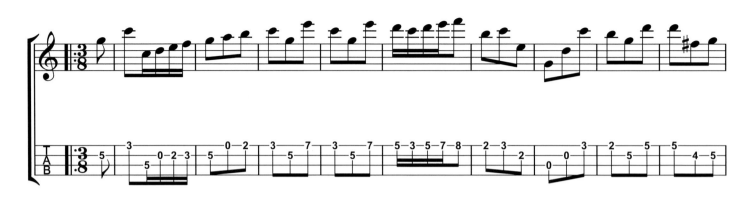

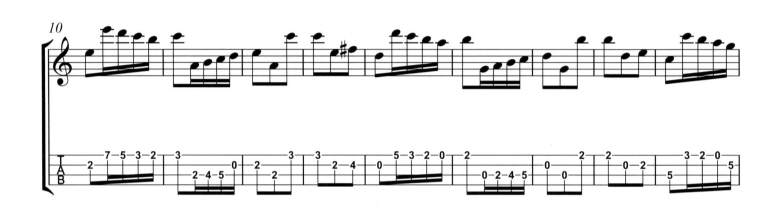

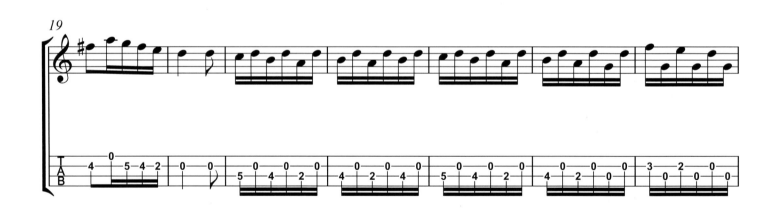

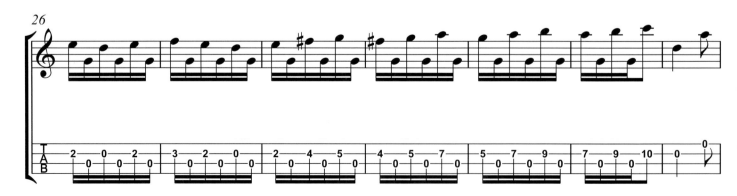

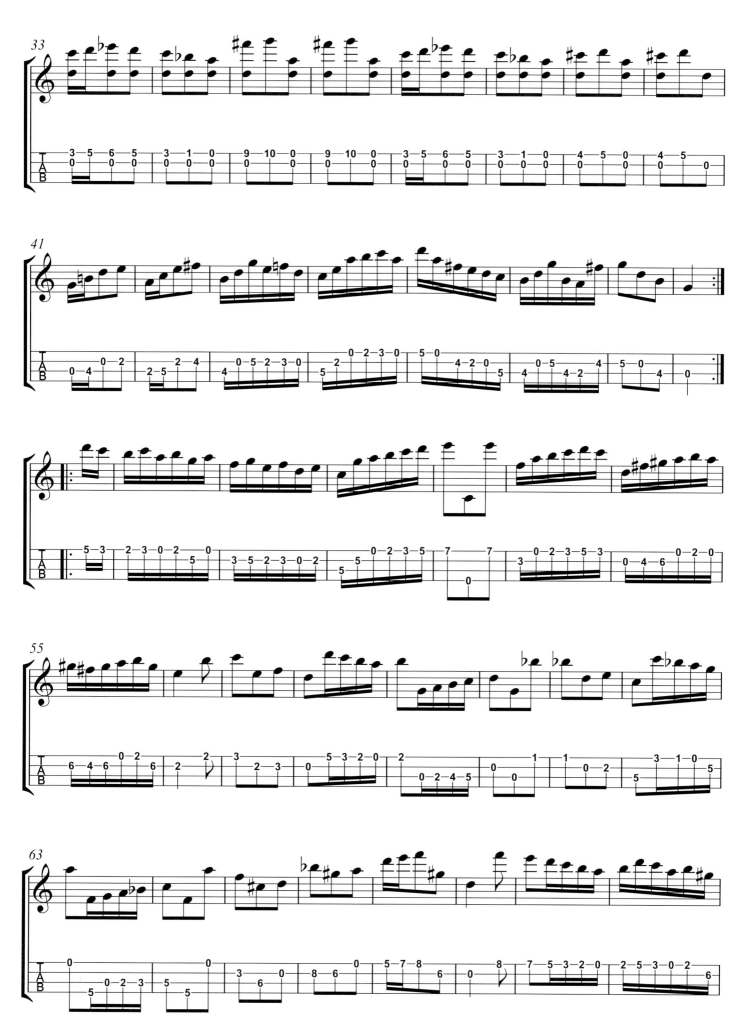

58

Rob MacKillop

"One of Scotland's finest musicians"
Celtic World

"A top-drawer player"
Early Music Today

"MacKillop displays dazzling virtuosity...the playing is exceptionally musical"
Sounding Strings

Rob MacKillop has recorded eight CDs of historical music, three of which reached the Number One position in the Scottish Classical Music Chart. In 2001 he was awarded a Churchill Fellowship for his research into medieval Scottish music, which led him to studying with Sufi musicians in Istanbul and Morocco. He broadcast an entire solo concert on BBC Radio 3 from John Smith's Square, London. He has presented academic papers at conferences in Portugal and Germany, and has been published many times. Rob has been active in both historical and contemporary music.

Three of Scotland's leading contemporary composers have written works for him, and he also composes new works himself. In 2004 he was Composer in Residence for Morgan Academy in Dundee, and in 2001 was Musician in Residence for Madras College in St. Andrews. He created and Directed the Dundee Summer Music Festival.

He worked as a Reader of schools literature for Oxford University Press, and as a reviewer for *Music Teacher*. He has also been Lecturer in Scottish Musical History at Aberdeen University, Dundee University, and at the Royal Scottish Academy of Music and Drama, and for five years worked as Musician In Residence to Queen Margaret University in Edinburgh. He has been a regular article writer for BMG magazine.

Rob plays banjo, guitar and ukulele, often with gut strings, plucking the strings with the flesh of his fingers, not the nails. This produces a warm and intimate sound, reminiscent of the old lute players.

Rob MacKillop is at the forefront of the revival of historical banjo styles, performing on period and modern instruments.

Skype or FaceTime Lessons in Banjo, Guitar and Ukulele. Details: RobMacKillop.net

Checkout www.MelBay.com for more editions by Rob MacKillop